The Wisdom of Meister Eckhart

Selected and edited by
Jan Stryz
With an introduction by
Arthur Versluis

Great Works of Christian Spirituality

New Grail

Library of Congress Cataloging-in-Publication Data
Eckhart, Meister, d. 1327
  [Sermons. English. Selections]
  The wisdom of Meister Eckhart / Selected and edited by Jan Stryz;
with an introduction by Arthur Versluis.
  81 p. cm.-- (Great works of Christian spirituality ; v. 1)
  Includes bibliographical references and index.
  ISBN 0-9650488-5-3 (alk. paper)   6/04
  1. Mysticism--Sermons. 2. Catholic Church--Sermons. 3. Sermons, English.
I. Stryz, Jan. II Versluis, Arthur, 1959- III. Title. IV. Series.

BV5082.3 .E3513 2003
252'.02--dc21
                                            2002035804

©Arthur Versluis and Jan Stryz 2003

All rights reserved. No part of this publication may be reproduced, stored in a retrieval system, or transmitted in any form or by any means, electronic, mechanical, photocopying, recording or otherwise, without the prior permission of the publisher.

New Grail Publishing
St. Paul, Minnesota

www.grailbooks.org

New Grail Publishing
P. O. Box 14285
St. Paul, Minnesota 55114

The Wisdom of Meister Eckhart

Contents
Introduction by Arthur Versluis . . . 1
The Secret Word . . . 17
God is Nothing . . . 23
The Eternal Birth . . . 24
Let Go of Everything . . . 28
God and the Soul . . . 33
Where Creature Stops, God Begins . . . 34
The Grail . . . 37
The True Light . . . 38
On the Spirit . . . 44
God Does Not Look Outside Himself . . . 46
On Angels . . . 47
Time and Eternity . . . 48
What is Conceived Where God Conceives Himself . . . 49
The Qualities of Intellect . . . 50
Prepare All Creatures to Return to God . . . 53
What is Prayer? . . . 55
The Soul Gives Birth to Itself . . . 57
The Seat of Happiness . . . 60
Leaving God for God . . . 64
On Detachment . . . 68
Index . . . 81

Volume I in *Great Works of Christian Spirituality*
Series Editor: Arthur Versluis
Volume Editor: Jan Stryz

The Wisdom of Meister Eckhart

Introduction by Arthur Versluis

Meister Eckhart (1260-1327) is quite arguably the greatest Christian mystic of all time. Of course, the word "mysticism" is vague and usually connotes visionary experiences, of which there is little trace in Eckhart. Still, with the possible exception of Dionysius the Areopagite, Eckhart is certainly the greatest exponent of the *via negativa*, or path of negation. The path of negation is that of absolute imageless transcendence, and this is at the heart of Eckhart's mysticism. But Eckhart expresses this path of negation in the most colorful and daring ways of anyone in the history of Christianity. In this collection of his work, we offer selections from his sermons that reveal just how extraordinary he was, and that are meant to offer a way into the tradition that he more than anyone else exemplifies.

Eckhart was born, probably to nobility, in Thuringia near Erfurt in about 1260. He most likely joined the Dominican priory at Erfurt in 1275, and it is quite possible that before 1280 he studied at Cologne, where Albertus Magnus was still teaching. By 1293, we know that Eckhart took part in disputations in Paris, and that by 1298 he was known as Prior of Erfurt and Vicar of Thuringia. By 1302, he had received the title "Meister," or Master, for his theological knowledge. And in 1303, he was elected to the position of Provincial of Saxony (including much of Northern Germany and Holland). In 1307, he became Vicar-General of Bohemia, and in 1310, Provincial of the Southern German province of Alemannia. By 1314, he was in charge of a convent at Strassburg, while carrying out his other official duties. In 1322 came the greatest honor of all, when he was called to Cologne to assume the chair once held by none other than Albertus Magnus himself.

But the Archbishop of Cologne at the time, Heinrich von Virneburg, was a sour Franciscan who was bitterly opposed to anything that resembled "mysticism," which he associated with heresy. In 1326, the archbishop instituted proceedings against Eckhart before the Inquisition for spreading dangerous doctrines among common folk. Because of his fame and reputation, Eckhart probably was not in danger of being burnt at the stake, but it became a nasty battle for him nonetheless. Several lists of supposedly incriminating statements were drawn up against him, which he refuted chiefly by showing that they were indeed orthodox and that his accusers simply didn't understand what they were impugning. On 13 February, 1327, Eckhart publicly declared that he was not a heretic, that what was attributed to him as heresy had been distorted or misunderstood, and that anything inadvertently heretical he had said he now retracted. The case continued, but Eckhart died before 1328. In 1329, some of Eckhart's work was denounced in a papal bull as heretical, ironically enough by a pope who had accumulated great wealth and who was himself denounced by a subsqurent pope as heretical!

This ill-considered and confused condemnation kept Eckhart from being more widely known for centuries to come, though he was influential for such subsequent figures as Heinrich Suso, Johannes Tauler, Nicholas of Cusa, the *Theologia Germanica*, and Angelus Silesius, and was rediscovered in the nineteenth century by Franz von Baader, the great theosopher in the tradition of Jacob Böhme (d. 1624). But Eckhart came into his own in the twentieth century, for as the West came into genuine contact with Asian religious traditions, notably Vedanta and Mahayana Buddhism, Eckhart's genius for apophatic or negative theology suddenly could be seen in a new light. If in the fourteenth century, he could be portrayed as heretical, by the twentieth century his daring insistence on the transcendent nature of the Godhead and of the spiritual awakening of the individual could be seen in a world context as the European parallel to Buddhist metaphysics.

The parallels between Meister Eckhart's thought and Mahayana Buddhism became more widely known with the publication of a book entitled *Mysticism: Christian and Buddhist* by D. T. Suzuki in 1957, and by Shizuteru Ueda in his book *Die Gottesgeburt in der Seele*, published in 1965. Suzuki in particular was keen to show "the closeness of Meister Eckhart's way of thinking to that of Mahayana Buddhism, especially of Zen Buddhism" (3). Suzuki spent the beginning of his study considering Eckhart's teachings concerning detachment and the "pure Nothing," because these and related concepts are very much akin to the concept of emptiness, or *shunyata*, in Buddhism. And without doubt, there are many other parallels between Eckhart's work and Zen Buddhism, so many that to this day Eckhart remains the subject of ever more comparisons between Christian mysticism and Buddhism, particularly in Japanese scholarship.

What is it in Eckhart's work that makes him so amenable to comparison with Buddhism or Vedanta? We may begin by considering the way Eckhart begins our selection entitled "The Secret Word": "Here in time we celebrate because the eternal birth that God the Father bears unceasingly in eternity is born now, in time and human nature. According to St. Augustine, this birth is always happening. But what does it profit me if it does not happen in me?" From the outset, it is clear that Eckhart has little to do with what we may call an historicist Christianity—that is, with a Christianity that emphasizes faith or belief without any inner process of regeneration or awakening. It is not enough only to believe this or that, according to Eckhart: we must realize what Eckhart here calls the "eternal birth" for ourselves. In other words, Eckhart insists above all that we directly experience spiritual illumination for ourselves, and that "the highest attainment in this life is to remain still and let God act and speak in us." He calls us to enter into the soul's hidden ground and to be reborn.

This process of rebirth takes place through the path known as apophatic, or negation, but could also be termed the path of transcendence. This path of transcendence is one that goes beyond the intellect; it is one in which the soul's spark, or *synteresis*, that inner transcendent faculty, perceives the divine within one in a way that can best be termed "unknowing." Eckhart explains that "There is more in this unknowing knowledge than in any ordinary understanding, for this unknowing lures you away from all understood things and from yourself. This is what Christ meant when he said: 'Whoever does not deny himself and leave father and mother and is not estranged from all these, is not worthy of me.' That is as though to say: whoever does not abandon creaturely externals can neither be conceived or born in this divine birth." Entering into this unknowing might also be called a kind of gnosis, or inner spiritual knowledge, though as Eckhart has it, "the height of gnosis is to know in agnosia." In *agnosia*, or unknowing, one realizes direct spiritual understanding for oneself.

The Christian path of transcendence takes its origin from Dionysius the Areopagite (ca. fifth century A.D.), whose treatises on the *via negativa* remain a cornerstone of Christian mysticism to this day. Eckhart explicitly draws upon Dionysius with some frequency, particularly concerning the divine Nothingness. Thus when Eckhart writes that "In unknowing knowing we know God, in forgetfulness of ourselves and all things up to the naked essence of the Godhead," it is in a passage that both begins and ends with references to Dionsyius. Yet let it not be thought that this unknowing knowing is without signs. Eckhart writes of this new birth that in it "God pours into the soul in such abundance of light that it floods the soul's ground, running into her powers and into the outward man as well. So it befell Paul when upon his journey God touched him with his light and spoke to him: the reflection of this light showed outwardly so that his companions saw it surrounding Paul like the saints." According to Eckhart, this unknowing knowing is the soul's becoming acclimated to God, and being filled with spiritual knowledge that is simultaneously love and joy. In all of this, Eckhart's work is very much in the lineage of Dionysius.

   Yet Eckhart is also extraordinary for his inventiveness and daringness of expression; he is not by any means a derivative author, but rather clearly writes directly from his own experience. Who can doubt that when he writes "God enjoys himself in all things," such an observation comes from Eckhart's own experience? But he also speaks explicitly of himself, as when he remarks that "My outer man enjoys creatures as creatures, like wine and bread and meat. But my inner man enjoys things not as creatures, but as the gift of God. And my inmost man enjoys them not as God's gift, but as eternity." This inner experience of God gives rise to Eckhart's understanding of the profound relation between creatures and God, for the contemplative realizes this relation directly for himself. Hence Eckhart observes that "Things perceived by my soul from without contain an outside element. But my perception of creatures in God contains God alone, for in God there is nothing but God. When I see all creatures in God I see nothing." It is as daring today as it was in his own time for Eckhart to speak openly of seeing all creatures in God, or of realizing God as the divine Nothing.

Still, it is often said, and I myself have occasionally thought, that Eckhart's work presents a view from the heights—breathtaking, to be sure, but without any clear directions on how we get to those heights ourselves. Yet a closer reading of his work reveals definite instructions on contemplative practice. He tells, for example, the story of a mathematician so engrossed in his mathematical studies that he did not even hear when he was challenged by a swordsman, who subsequently cut off the philosopher's head! If this is how engrossed someone in the natural sciences might be, how much more must the contemplative be engrossed in his practice! Eckhart reminds us that "A master says, 'To achieve this interior act, one must gather all one's powers into one corner of the soul, where, secreted from images and forms, one can work.' We must attain an oblivion and unknowing. This unknowing is not ignorance, but transformed knowledge; it is by knowing that we get to this unknowing." His work reveals a contemplative path that goes beyond what we usually understand by "contemplation"—that is, thinking—and into what we may call "meditation," by this meaning a sitting practice very much akin to what we find in Zen and most other forms of Mahayana Buddhism.

Eckhart calls us to "to root ourselves in this same ground of contemplation . . . True, there is motion, but no more than one: it comes from God and goes back to God . . . in this activity we are in the state of contemplation in God." We are, in this endeavour, called to

> above all, lay no claim to anything. Let go of yourself and let God act for you and in you as he pleases. This work is his, this Word is his, this birth is his, and all you are, as well. For you have abandoned yourself and are gone out of all your faculties and personal nature. God installs himself in your nature when, self-bereft of all belongings, you take to the desert. There is 'a voice crying in the wilderness,' as it is written. Let this eternal voice cry on in you at its sweet will, and become a desert in respect to self and creatures.

I have let Eckhart speak for himself here because it is clear even from these few excerpts that he is encouraging us on a specific contemplative path, a path toward transcendence beyond all images and earthly attachments, a rooting in the groundless ground of all things, the Godhead even beyond God himself.

This contemplative practice of Eckhart is prayer, but not in any discursive sense. For Eckhart, prayer is "glorying in pure being." It is transcendence, a freedom from all apparent division between subject and object, an entry into the "river and fount of Godhead." In contemplative prayer, there is no one to ask or hear a question, Eckhart tells us, and when one "flows forth" after immersion in this state, "all creatures speak God." This movement between awareness in the inner ground and movement is akin to the shift, in Buddhist meditation practice, from deep contemplation to active or walking meditation or to put it another way, from deep *samadhi* (contemplative absorption) to dynamic *samadhi*. In contemplative absorption, Eckhart tells us, "I alone take all creatures out of their sense into my mind and make them one in me. When I go back into the ground, into the depths, into the well-spring of the Godhead, no one will ask me from where I came or where I went. No one will miss me, for there God unbecomes."

We should note here the characteristic distinction that Eckhart makes between the Godhead and God, which corresponds to the distinction on the human level between deep contemplative absorption (the Godhead) and dynamic absorption when one conveys this realization in the world actively (God). Eckhart puts this distinction this way: "And why do [all creatures] not speak the Godhead? Everything in the Godhead is one, and of that there is nothing to be said. God works; the Godhead does no work. In the Godhead there is nothing to do; there is no activity. It never envisaged any work. God and Godhead are as different as active and inactive." It is absolutely clear that Eckhart, exactly like Jacob Böhme and John Pordage after him, is here drawing on his own direct experience. He does not offer a narrative, as Pordage often does, but nonetheless it is clear that he has experienced this distinction between God and the Godhead, or to put it another way, between deep and active contemplation.

This "movement" between active and deep contemplation corresponds to our emanation into existence and our breakthrough return to the divine origin. Eckhart expresses this "movement" in many ways, as here, when he tells us that

While I yet stood in my first cause I had no God and I was my own; I willed nothing and wanted nothing, for I was conditionless being, the knower of myself in divine truth. Then I wanted myself and nothing else. What I willed I was and what I was I willed. I was free from God and all things. But when I escaped from my free will to take on my created nature, then I acquired a God, for before creatures came into existence, God was not God. He was what he was. When creatures came into existence, God was not God in himself, but he was God in creatures.

This "God in creatures" is not pantheism, but is an expression of what in human terms is active contemplation, or the realization of the divine in all things as an "extension" of deep contemplation.

But creatures cannot be satisfied with realization of God as God, because this still implies dualism. Thus Eckhart writes that "God as God is not the final goal of creatures. If a flea had intellect and could plumb the eternal abyss of God's being, out of which it came, then not God and all God is could fulfill that flea. Therefore we pray we may be quit of God and get the truth and enjoy eternity, for the highest angel and the soul are all the same yonder where I was and willed that I was and was that I willed." In deep contemplation, God as God—that is, as a conceptual designation for being or consciousness somehow separate from us—cannot satisfy our deepest longing for realization. Thus we must be "quit of God" and enter into what precedes and transcends the division between God and creatures, into the transcendence that Eckhart refers to as the Godhead.

Eckhart lays great emphasis on this point, and goes so far as to write that "Why I pray God to rid me of God is because conditionless being is above God and above distinction. It was there I was myself, there I willed myself and knew myself to make this man. In this sense I am my own cause, both of my eternal nature and my temporal nature. In my birth all things were born, and I was the cause of my own self and all things." In other words, in the deepest contemplative experience, one enters into "conditionless being" that is prior to and beyond all distinctions, beyond therefore the distinct concept of God, so that "I" become "my own cause." If we remain in a self-other relation to God, we remain trapped in discursive reason and are incapable of going beyond this subject-object division.

Eckhart, in such daring passages, is urging us to go beyond this apparent subject-object division, just as he has done, and just as St. Paul did. Eckhart remarks that "I will put into plain words what St. Paul means by wishing to depart from God. Man's last and highest leave-taking is leaving God for God. St. Paul left God for God: he left everything he could give or take of God, every concept of God. In leaving these, he left God for God since God remained to him in his essential self, not as a concept of himself, or as an acquired thing, but God in his essential actuality." For this reason, Eckhart adds, St. Paul revealed himself to be perfect, that is, to have left behind the self-other distinction and to have realized for himself what is beyond the concept of God. One who has done that is known, Eckhart tells us, as a "true man," that is, as someone who has realized what the true purpose is of human life.

The true purpose of human life is to be like God, which is to say, to realize absolute detachment. Eckhart's treatise on detachment is rightfully his most famous, and for this reason we have included it nearly in its entirety. For Eckhart, detachment is the highest of all virtues and attainments; for to realize detachment is to realize for oneself the nature of God. To be full of creatures is to be empty of God; and to be empty of creatures is to be full of God, Eckhart tells us. To be empty of creatures means detachment, and

The more we are disposed to receive the inflowing God, the happier we will be; perfect receptivity gives perfect felicity. Now one can make oneself receptive to God only through uniformity with God; the degree of uniformity corresponds to the degree of receptivity. Uniformity comes of subjection to God, and the more one is subject to creatures the less one is uniform with God. But the detached heart, devoid of all creatures, utterly subject to and uniform with God, is wholly receptive to his divine inflow. Hence St. Paul exhorts us to "Put on Christ"—that is, uniformity with Christ.

What is the object of detachment? It is "neither this nor that;" it is to realize the Nothing at our own center, so that God can will through us.

Conventional notions of God Eckhart discards out of hand. God, he writes, "does not see in time, nor is his outlook subject to renewal." Eckhart continues:

Isidorus argues this in his book on the Arch-Good. He says that people are always asking what God did before he created the heavens and the earth, and how there arose in God the new will to make creatures. His reply is that no new will arose in God, for even if creatures might not have existed before as they do now, yet they have existed from eternity in God and in the mind of God. God did not create the heavens and earth as we imagine when we say in our words, 'Let them be!'; rather, creatures are all spoken in his eternal Word.

Eckhart thus completely dismisses the conventional notion of biblical creationism, for God did not create the way that human beings tend to imagine, in a dualistic way. Further, God does not answer petitionary prayer as a result of a cause in time. Rather, if a prayer is answered, it is because that answer existed already in eternity before you were born, just as if a prayer is not answered, because it is foolish or misguided, it is because this denial existed in eternity prior to your asking it. Still, "men's prayers and virtuous works are not in done in vain. Whoever does well is well rewarded, though God does stay all the while in motionless detachment."

Contemplative practice is at heart the practice of detachment from all things and so "there is none happier than one who exists in absolute detachment . . . . Detachment is the best of all, for it cleanses the soul, clarifies the mind, kindles the heart and wakens the spirit; it quickens desire, enhances the virtue-giving intuition of God, and separating us from creatures, unites us with God." This detachment is realized through deep contemplation, entering into the formless essence that precedes creation and all separation. The detached heart prays for nothing, because it desires nothing except unity with God. It enters into the uncreated, and "attaining this, the soul loses her identity. God absorbs her so that as self she becomes nothing, just as the sunlight swallows the dawn." This is the realization of absolute detachment, the transcendence of all distinctions and the realization of union with the Godhead, the ultimate purpose of human life.

Near the end of his treatise, Eckhart quotes Augustine, who wrote that "The soul has a private door into divine nature, where all things become nothing to her." "This door on earth is absolute detachment," Eckhart commented. The whole of Eckhart's work may be seen as his showing the way to this door. If some of his work is controversial still, if his mode of expression is bold, set that aside until later, for with repeated reading and contemplative practice, much in his work becomes clearer. For what matters in the end is not our disputations or parsing of words, but whether we find this "private door into divine nature" and pass through it for ourselves. It is to this end, to our passing through this door, that the whole of Eckhart's work is devoted, and to this end that this little book is dedicated as well.

Vale.

Selected Bibliography

Raymond Blakney, *Meister Eckhart: A Modern Translation*, (New York: Harper, 1941)
Robert K. C. Forman, *Meister Eckhart: Mystic as Theologian*, (Shaftesbury: Element, 1991)
Bernard McGinn, *Meister Eckhart: Teacher and Preacher*, (New York: Paulist P, 1986)
M. O'C. Walshe, *Meister Eckhart: Sermons and Treatises*, Vols. I-III, (London: Watkins, 1981)
Franz Pfeiffer, *Meister Eckhart*, (Leipzig: 1857), translated by C. de B. Evans, (London: Watkins, 1924)
Josef Quint and Ernst Benz, *Meister Eckhart: Die deutschen und lateinischen Werke*, (Stuttgart: Kohlhammer, 1936 ff.)

Note on our text: This version of Eckhart's sermons was adapted from a comparison of modern translations of Eckhart's work, beginning with C. de B. Evans's translation of Franz Pfeiffer's 1857 work. We have made every effort to be faithful to Eckhart's meaning.

The Wisdom of Meister Eckhart

The Secret Word

Here in time we celebrate because the eternal birth that God the Father bears unceasingly in eternity is born now, in time and human nature. According to St. Augustine, this birth is always happening. But what does it profit me if it does not happen in me?

A wise man said: "When all things lay in the midst of silence, then there descended into me from on high, from the royal throne, a secret word." This sermon concerns that word.

First we will consider the phrase: "In the midst of silence, there was spoken in me a secret word."

—"But, sir, where is the silence and where is the word spoken?"

It is in the purest, noblest part of the soul, in her ground and very essence. That is the silent center where no creature or image has ever penetrated. There the soul has no activity or understanding, and thus no image of herself or any creature. Here alone is rest and habitation for this birth, where God the Father can speak his Word, for it is intrinsically receptive of nothing save the divine essence. Here God enters the soul with his all, not merely with a part.

Creatures cannot enter the soul, nor can the soul know anything about a creature the image of which she has not willingly absorbed. An image is a thing that the soul creates with her powers, by means of which she approaches creatures. But an image received in this way must enter from without through the senses. Consequently there is nothing so unknown to the soul as herself. As one philosopher says, the soul can neither create nor absorb an image of herself.

Now you must know that the interior of the soul is free from both means and images; that is why God can unite with her freely without form or appearance. Surely, any power we might attribute to a master, God possesses without measure. The wiser and more powerful the master, the more immediately and simply his work is effected. Man requires many instruments for his external works, and much preparation is needed before he can bring them forth as he has imagined them. More exalted are the angels, who need fewer means and images for their works. The highest Seraph has but a single image. He seizes as a unity all that his inferiors regard as manifold. But God needs no image and has no image: God works in the soul without image, likeness or means. This no creature can do.

—"How does God the Father give birth to his Son in the soul: like creatures, in image and likeness?"

No, by my faith! It occurs just as he gives him birth in eternity, and not otherwise.

—"Well, but how does he give him birth there?"

See. God the Father has perfect insight into himself, profound and thorough knowledge of himself through himself, not by means of any image. Thus God the Father gives birth to his Son in the very oneness of the divine nature. In the same way, God the Father gives birth to his Son in the ground and essence of the soul, and thus he unites himself with her. Were any image present there would not be real union, and in real union lies our beatitude.

Now you might say: "But there is nothing innate in the soul but images." This is not true! If it were, then the soul could never be happy, for no creature can provide us with perfect happiness. Union with God is the highest happiness and final goal; it is his will and nature to be the alpha and omega of all. Therefore you must dwell in the ground of your soul, where God will join you to his essence without the medium of any image.

The second point to consider is what you should do to bring this birth to pass in yourself. Is it better to take action by imagining and thinking about God, or should you keep still and wait so that God can speak and act in you? At the same time, note that only the good and perfect, who have so absorbed the essence of virtue that it emanates from them naturally, are fit to receive this act of God. Above all there must live in them the worthy life and lofty teaching of our Lord Jesus Christ.

Such know that the highest attainment in this life is to remain still and let God act and speak in us. When the soul withdraws her powers from bodily forms and functions, then this Word is spoken. The more completely you can withdraw your faculties and forget the things and images you have taken in, the more susceptible you are to this act. If only you could be suddenly unaware of things, and even of your very existence, as was St. Paul when he said: "Whether in the body or out of the body I know not; God knoweth!" His spirit had so entirely absorbed the faculties that it had forgotten the body. Memory no longer functioned, nor understanding, nor the senses; vital heat and energy were suspended so that the body was sustained during the three days that he neither ate or drank.

God works without instruments or images. The freer you are from images, the more receptive you are to his interior operation. God scorns to work among images.

Now you might say: "What does God do without images in the ground and essence?" That I do not know; my soul-powers can receive only in images.

Since all images enter from without, this knowledge is concealed from my soul, and that is best for her. Not knowing makes her wonder and eager to pursue what she is certain is there, but the nature of which is a mystery to her. Once a person knows the reason for something, he tires of it and looks for something new. The soul is constant only to this knowledge shrouded in mystery, which keeps her seeking.

Concerning this, the wise man said: "In the middle of the night, when all things were in quiet silence, there was spoken to me a hidden word." What does he mean by a word that was hidden? The nature of a word is to reveal what is hidden. It shone before me, intending to reveal knowledge of God. Hence it is called a word. But what is was remained hidden from me. Because it is hidden, one must always pursue it; we are meant to yearn and sigh for it.

When St. Paul returned after having been caught up into the third heaven where God was made known to him and where he beheld all things, he had forgotten nothing, but it was so deep down in his ground that his intellect could not reach it; it was veiled from him. Therefore, he was obliged to search for it inside himself. It is not outside; it is wholly within. Convinced of this, he declared: "I am sure that neither death nor any affliction can separate me from what I find within me."

St. Augustine says: "I am conscious of something within me that plays before my soul and is as a light dancing in front of it; were this brought to steadiness and perfection in me it would surely be eternal life!" It hides yet it shows. It comes, but after the manner of a thief, with intent to steal all things from the soul. Revealing a glimpse of itself, it decoys the soul towards its mystery so as to rob the soul of itself. As the prophet says: "Lord, take from them their spirit and give them instead thy spirit."

Now perhaps you will say: "But, Sir, you wish to change the natural course of the soul! It is her nature to take in things through the senses by means of images. Would you upset this arrangement?"

No, but how do know what nobility God has bestowed on human nature, what perfections are yet uncatalogued and even undiscovered? Those who have written of the soul's nobility have gone no further than their natural intelligence could carry them; they never entered her ground, so that much remained unknown to them.

Mark now the fruit and use of this mysterious Word and that darkness into which it comes. Not only is the Son born in the darkness of the heavenly Father; you too are born there of the heavenly Father, and to you also he gives power. Observe its great use. No truth learned through the intellect by any master, now or ever, can be interpreted at all according to this knowledge, this ground. There is more in this unknowing knowledge than in any ordinary understanding, for this unknowing lures you away from all understood things and from yourself. This is what Christ meant when he said: "Whoever does not deny himself and leave father and mother and is not estranged from all these, is not worthy of me." That is as though to say: whoever does not abandon creaturely externals can neither be conceived or born in this divine birth.

I believe—no, I am certain—that the person established in this cannot be separated from God. I hold that he cannot lapse into mortal sin. I hold that he cannot willingly commit, or even consent to, a venial sin, whether in himself or another. He is so strongly drawn and habituated to this way, that he could never turn to any other.

May the God who has been born again as man assist us in this birth, continually helping us, weak mortals, to be born again in him as God. Amen.

God is Nothing

Dionysius says: God is Nothing. By this he means that God is incomprehensible as Nothing: God is super-essential, super-rational, super-intelligible. Dionysius teaches that the divine being is not comprehensible in any sense, not even to the angels.

Thus the height of gnosis is to know in agnosia.

To know God is to know him as unknowable. As the master puts it: if I must speak of God, then I will say that God is in no way reachable or graspable, and that I know nothing else about him.

Whatever Dionysius conceives, God far transcends it. There is no knowing him by likeness.

In unknowing knowing we know God, in forgetfulness of ourselves and all things up to the naked essence of the Godhead.

Dionysius exhorted one of his disciples: Friend, cease from all activity and empty yourself of self that you may commune with the sovereign God.
Pray God we may seek him so that we shall find him, never again to lose him. Amen.

The Eternal Birth

Granting that God is in all things as mind, and is more innate to things than they are to themselves, and granting that God acts wherever he is, speaking his Word, then note in what respect the soul is better suited than other rational creatures to God's operation.

God is in all things as being, activity, power. But he is procreative in the soul alone, for though every creature is a vestige of God, the soul is the natural image of God. This image is perfected and adorned in the eternal birth. No creature but the soul is susceptible to this birth. What comes to you through this brings true being and stability, and whatever you seek outside of this perishes. This birth alone gives life; all else corrupts. Further, in this birth you participate in the divine influx and all its gifts. This is not received by creatures wherein God's image is not found.

Another question is: If this birth happens in the ground of the soul, then it happens alike in sinner and saint, so what good is it to me? The ground of nature is the same in both, and even in hell the nobility of the soul's nature exists eternally.

In this birth God pours into the soul in such abundance of light, that it floods the soul's ground, running into her powers and into the outward man as well. So it befell Paul when upon his journey God touched him with his light and spoke to him: the reflection of this light showed outwardly so that his companions saw it surrounding Paul like the saints.

No sinner can receive this light, nor is he worthy to, being filled with the darkness of sin. As John says, "The darkness neither receives nor comprehends the light." The avenues by which the light would enter are choked by guile and darkness. Because this light cannot shine in sinners, this birth cannot occur in them.

Then comes the question: If God the Father labors only in the ground and essence of the soul, not in her powers, what do the powers have to do with it? God works to bring the soul and all her powers into himself. Here, the soul is scattered abroad among her powers and dissipated in the act of each: the power of seeing in the eye, the power of hearing in the ear, the power of tasting in the tongue. Scattered forces are imperfect, and thus her powers are enfeebled for their interior work. For her interior work to be effective, she must recall her powers into one act.

St. Augustine says, "The soul is where she loves rather than where she animates the body." Consider the heathen philosopher who studied mathematics. He was sitting by the embers making calculations when a man brandishing a sword came along and, not knowing it was the master, cried out: "Quick, tell me your name or be killed!" The master was too absorbed to see or hear his enemy, so after repeating his demand several times, the man cut off the philosopher's head. And this concentration was just in service to mere natural science. How much more does it profit us to withdraw from things in order to concentrate our powers on perceiving and knowing the one immortal truth.

A master says, "To achieve this interior act, one must gather all one's powers into one corner of the soul, where, secreted from images and forms, one can work." We must attain an oblivion and unknowing. This unknowing is not ignorance, but transformed knowledge; it is by knowing that we get to this unknowing.

Thus our passivity is superior to our activity. One authority holds that that the sense of hearing is much nobler than that of sight, for we learn wisdom more by ear than eye. Hearing draws in more; seeing leads out more. In eternal life we a far happier in our ability to hear than to see, because the act of hearing the eternal Word is in me, whereas the act of seeing goes forth from me. Hearing, I am receptive; seeing, I am active.

Our bliss lies not in being active, but in being receptive to God. God's work is more excellent than mine. Out of love, God set our happiness in acceptance, for we receive far more than we give. Further, each divine gift prepares us for the next by increasing our capacity and desire for some new and greater gift. Some theologians say that the soul is symmetrical with God in this respect. For as God is infinite in giving, so the soul is infinite in receiving or conceiving. As the soul is as profound in her capacity to accept as God is omnipotent to act, hence she is transformed with God and in God.

Let Go of Everything

Man possesses an active intellect, a passive intellect and a potential intellect. Active intellect is ever doing something for the honor and glory of God, whether in God or in creatures. But when God undertakes the work, the mind must be passive. Now, before the work is begun by the mind and finished by God, the spirit has prevision of it, potential knowledge of its happening. This is the meaning of potential intellect, which, however, is often neglected and does not bear fruit. When the mind is exerting itself in real earnest, God interests himself in the mind and its work, and then the soul sees and experiences God. But since the uninterrupted vision of God is intolerable to the soul in this body, God withdraws from the soul from time to time. As it is said: "A little while you see me, and again a little while and you do not see me."

When our Lord took his three disciples with him up the mountain and showed them the transfiguration of his body by union with the Godhead—which we also will have in our archetypal body—straightaway Peter, beholding it, wanted to remain there always. Wherever we find true goodness, we do not want to leave it. Intuition discovers it, then love follows, and memory, and all the soul. And our Lord, knowing this, hides himself sometimes. Were the soul conscious of the goodness that is God without mediation or interruption, she would never be able to leave it to influence the body.

Thus it befell Paul. Had he remained there a hundred years, where he knew the good, he would never have returned to his body. He would have forgotten it completely. Seeing that the good is foreign to this life, God veils it and unveils it when he chooses, knowing what is best for you, like a trusty physician. It is in his hands to show or not, according to his knowledge of what you can endure.

But you will raise the question: If this requires a mind free from images and activity, though both are natural to its powers, then what about outward works such as works of charity and teaching and comforting those in need? Do these interfere with our attainment of the good? Are we to be deprived of this great good because we are engaged in charities?

The answer is this: the one is perfect, the other very profitable. Mary was praised for choosing the best, but Martha's life was very useful, serving Christ and his disciples. St. Thomas says the active life is better than the life of contemplation, so far as we actually spend in charity the income we derive from contemplation. It is all the same thing; we have but to root ourselves in this same ground of contemplation to make it fruitful in works, and the object of contemplation is achieved. True, there is motion, but no more than one: it comes from God and goes back to God. Even so in this activity we are in the state of contemplation in God. The one is centered in the other and perfects it. God's purpose in the union of contemplation is fruitfulness in works. For in contemplation you serve yourself alone, but the many are served in good works.

You may object: "But what of that silence you said so much about? All of these acts mean images galore. Each one has its appropriate image, whether it is teaching one or comforting another or arranging this or that, so what quiet can I find in this? If the mind sees and formulates and the will wills and memory holds it fast, doesn't all this require ideas?"

Let me explain. We were speaking just now of the active intellect and the passive intellect. Active intellect abstracts the images of outward things, stripping them of matter and of accidents, and introduces them to the passive intellect, begetting their mental images therein. And the passive intellect, made pregnant by the active in this way, knows and cherishes these things with the help of active intellect. Passive intellect cannot keep on knowing things unless the active intellect keeps on enlightening it. Now what the active intellect does for the natural man, that and far more does God do for the solitary soul. He turns out active intellect, installing himself in its stead and assuming its duties.

Your active intellect cannot have two ideas together, but has first one and then the other. But when God acts in lieu of your active intellect, he engenders many images together in one point. Suppose God prompts you to some one good deed; your mind is immediately set on good in general. All your potential for good takes shape and comes to your mind, concentrated in one point. Clearly this is not the work of your own intellect, which lacks the perfection and plenitude for it. Rather, it is the work and product of him who possesses all forms at once within himself. Know then, that the ideas behind these acts are not your own; they belong to the author of your nature, who has planted in you both their energy and form. Lay no claim to them, for they are his, not yours. True, you receive them temporally, but they are gotten and born of God beyond time, in eternity above images.

Above all, lay no claim to anything. Let go of yourself and let God act for you and in you as he pleases. This work is his, this Word is his, this birth is his, and all you are, as well. For you have abandoned yourself and are gone out of all your faculties and personal nature. God installs himself in your nature when, self-bereft of all belongings, you take to the desert. There is "a voice crying in the wilderness," as it is written. Let this eternal voice cry on in you at its sweet will, and become a desert in respect to self and creatures.

You might ask: "But what must one do to become this desert, void of self and creatures? Should one stay waiting for God all the time and do nothing oneself, or should one do something in the meantime, such as praying or reading or going to church or studying the Bible? Not, of course, engaging in the mere outward forms of these things, but experiencing them inwardly, as from God. Besides, don't we miss something by neglecting these things?"

My answer is this: Outward works were instituted for the purpose of directing the outer man to God and training him to spiritual life, and to keep him from straying away from self to external things. That way, when God decides to work in him, he shall find him close at hand, and not first have to fetch him back from things gross and alien. The greater the pleasure in external things, the harder work it is to leave them; the stronger the love, the sharper the pain when it comes to parting.

All pious practices—praying, reading, singing, watching, fasting, penance, or whatever discipline it be—were contrived to catch and keep us from things alien and ungodly. But during the time that a man has genuine experience of the interior life, then let him boldly drop all outward disciplines.

God and the Soul

"God is love, and he who dwells in love dwells in God and God in him." This is the epistle we read at Mass, and it is St. John speaking.

God loves my soul so much that his very life and being depend upon his loving me, whether he would or not. To stop God loving me would be to rob him of his Godhood, for God is love no less than he is truth. As he is good, so is he love as well.

Certain theologians mantained that the love which is within us is the Holy Spirit, but this is false. For the bodily food we take is changed into us, but the spiritual food we receive changes us into itself. Hence, divine love is not preserved in us; otherwise, there would be two. Divine love preserves us in itself as one in the same.

Where two grow one, one loses its nature. Therefore, for God and the soul to be one, the soul has to lose her own life and nature. They are one as regards what is left.

Where Creature Stops, God Begins

"In this was manifested the love of God toward us that he sent his only-begotten Son into the world that we might live with the Son." That is, "in and through the Son."

If a mighty king had a beautiful daughter and gave her to a poor man's son, every member of his family would rise in rank and become ennobled. Thus one learned master says:'"By God becoming man the whole human race has been ennobled and exalted; thus we should rejoice greatly that Christ our brother has ascended above the angels and sits at the right hand of the Father." This is well-said, but I set little store by it. What does it profit me that my brother is rich, if I am poor, or that he is wise, if I am a fool?

I maintain something more significant: God not only became man, he assumed human nature. Philosophers agree that all men are of equal rank by nature. But I make bold to say that every good thing possessed by the saints and by Mary, God's mother, and by Christ in his human nature, is also mine in this same nature.

You will ask: "If I already possess in this nature all that Christ does in his humanity, why do we set Christ so high and honor him as our Lord and

God?"—Because he was a messenger from God to us, bringing us our happiness. The happiness he brought us was our own.

Another, even more difficult thing I say: To subsist immediately in this pure nature you must be so wholly dead to personal nature that you hold the same good will towards someone across the seas whom you have never seen, as you do to your own near and familiar friend. Secondly, you must be pure in heart, and only the heart that has exterminated creaturehood is pure. And thirdly, you must be free from *not*.

To the question "What burns in hell?", theologians reply with one accord: "self-will." But I maintain: *not* burns in hell. Here is a simile. Suppose I take a burning coal and put it in my hand. If I say the coal is burning me, I do it great injustice. Precisely what burns me is *not*, because the coal has something in it that my hand has not. It is this absence that burns me. If my hand contained what the coal is, it would possess the fire-nature. In that case, all the fire that ever burned might be taken and heaped upon my hand without its burning me.

Likewise, because God and those who are in sight of God have in them something pertaining to real happiness that those who are apart from God have not, it follows that this *not* alone torments the souls in hell more than personal will or any fire. To the extent that *not* inheres in you, you are imperfect.

Further, my text says: "God sent his only-begotten Son into the world." By this is meant not the external world, but the inner world. As surely as the Father by his simple nature begets the Son innately, so he begets him in the innermost recesses of the mind, the inner world. Here God's ground is my ground and my ground God's ground.

Out of this innermost ground your works should be wrought without motive. Indeed, as long as you do your works to attain the kingdom of heaven, or God, or your own eternal happiness, all is not well with you. It may be tolerable, but it is not the best. For he who seeks God under settled forms lays hold of the the form while missing the God concealed in it. But he who seeks God in no special guise lays hold of him as he is in himself, and "lives with the Son," and is the life himself.

We might question life for a thousand years: "Why do you live?" It would only say, if it replied at all, "I live because I live." For life lives in a ground of its own, and wells up out of its own. It lives without a cause, for it lives itself. And if anyone asked a proper man, one who works his own ground, "Why do you work?", he too would say, "I work because I work."

Where creature stops, there God begins. All God wants of you is for you to go out of yourself in respect of your creatureliness, and let God be God in you. The smallest of creaturely images that ever takes shape in you is as big as God. How so? Because it shuts out the whole of God. As soon as this image appears, God disappears with all his Godhood. As this image fades out, God comes in.

The Grail

My quotation from Ecclesiastes 50:10, "a golden vessel, massive and firm, adorned with every precious stone," can be applied to St. Augustine or to any virtuous soul.

Every cup has two qualities: it receives and holds. The spiritual vessel differs from the physical. The wine is in the cup, not the cup in the wine, though the wine is not in the cup as it is in the body, for if it were we would not be able to drink it. It is different with the spiritual vessel. Everything received in this is in the cup and the cup in it, and is the cup itself. All this spiritual cup receives is its own nature.

According to the scriptures, "No man knows the Father but the Son," and hence if you want to know God you have to be not merely like the Son; you have to be the very Son himself. Some people think to see God with their eyes as they would see a cow, and they expect to love him as they would love a cow. This you love for its milk and cheese—for its profit to yourself. Even so, those who love God with an eye to outward riches or inner consolation do not really love God, but their own personal advantage.

As I said just now that St. Augustine can be compared to a golden vessel, closed on the underside and open to the sky, so should you be as well. If you would stand with St. Augustine and the communion of saints, then close your heart to everything created and be open to God as he is in himself.

Be "firm and steady," the same in good fortune and misfortune. And be "set with all the precious stones," a treasury of all the virtues that come naturally pouring out of you. Traverse all the virtues and, transcending them, tap virtue only at its source, where it is one with the divine nature.

The True Light

A statement is made in St. Luke's narrative about St. Paul: "Paul rose from the ground with open eyes and seeing nothing." The words are open to four interpretations. One is, that when he rose up from the ground he was gazing wide-eyed at nothing, and that nothing was God. Another is that when he got up he saw nothing but God. The third, that he saw nothing but God in all things. The fourth, that in the divine vision he beheld all things as nothing.

He says, "A light from heaven shone round about him." A master says that in this light all the soul-powers—the outward senses we see and hear with as well as the inner senses we call thoughts—are exalted. Above thought comes the intellect as seeker. She goes about looking, casting her net here and there, gaining and losing. Above inellect the seeker there is another intellect which does not seek but rests in its pure and simple essence in the realm of light. In this light all the soul-powers are exalted. Senses rise to thoughts. How high, how fathomless these are, no one knows but God and the soul.

"In the encircling light he fell to earth, and his eyes being unsealed, he beheld all things as nothing." And beholding all things as nothing he was beholding God.

Note here what the soul says in the Book of Love: "By night in my bed I sought him my soul loves; I sought him and I found him not." This means that she sought him in a place that was too limited, belonging to the world below—her bed. God's entire creation is too confined. She said: "I sought him all night through." The sun is shining in the night, but is screened from view. By day it eclipses all other lights. So it is with the light of God; it puts out any other light.

All our creaturely expectations are night. Nothing we find in a creature is more than a shadow. Even the highest angel's light, exalted though it is, does not illumine the soul. All but the first light is darkness.

By night the soul cannot find God. "I rose and sought him all about, I scoured the broadways and the alleys. The watchmen (angels) found me, and I asked them: 'Have you seen him whom my soul loves?' " But they did not answer, perhaps because they could not apprehend him.

"I passed by a little and found him my soul loves." The little that she missed him by has often been the burden of my teaching. He to whom mortal things are not all trivial and as nothing shall not find God. When God pours into and informs the soul, and you take him as a light or a state or a boon, or whatever you know about him, that God is not. We have to transcend the little, discard the adventitious and perceive God as one.

We often say, "him my soul loves," but the soul does not name her love. There are four reasons for this. One is that God is nameless. God is beyond all name; none can express him. A second reason is that on swooning away into God for love, the soul is conscious of nothing but love. She fondly imagines that everyone knows him like that. She is amazed that anyone would find him anything but love alone. Third, she has no time to name him. Love does not leave her any time to use another word. Fourth, perhaps she thinks he has no other name but love. In love she pronounces all names.

"Paul rose from the ground wide-eyed, beholding nothing." I cannot see what is one. God is nothing and God is one. What is something is nothing as well. What God is, he is wholly. Dionysius says that God is above being, above life, above light. He does not call God any of these, but makes him out to be something I do not know that far transcends them. Anything that can enter your sight or your understanding, is not God, for God is neither this nor that. Whoever says God is here or there, do not believe.

God is the true light. To see it one has to be blind and strip God naked of things. A master says that to argue about God from any sort of likeness is to argue falsely about him. But to argue about God from nothing is to argue soundly. When the soul has become one by discarding herself altogether, then she finds God as in nothing.

It appeared to one soul as in a dream (it was a waking dream) that the soul became big with nothing, like a pregnant woman, and in that nothing God was born, the fruit of the nothing. God was born in the nothing.

Therefore it says, "He arose from the earth wide-eyed, gazing at nothing." He had a vision of God where there are no creatures. He beheld all creatures as nothing for he had the whole essence of creatures in him. He is the all-containing essence.

A second meaning of the phrase "he saw nothing" is this. According to our masters, any perception of externals entails some inroad by them, an impression at least. To get some idea of a thing, such as a stone, I do not take into my mind the grossest part of it. That I leave outside. As it exists in the ground of my soul, where it is at its noblest and best, it is merely an idea.

Things perceived by my soul from without contain an outside element. But my perception of creatures in God contains God alone, for in God there is nothing but God. When I see all creatures in God I see nothing. He saw God, where all creatures are nothing.

A third reason he saw nothing is that the Nothing was God. A master says, creatures in God are as nothing for he has in him the whole essence of creatures. He says there is nothing under to God, however near it might be to him, that does not have some alien taint. He says that an angel knows himself and God without means. Into other things he knows there come an outside element, however slight. If we are to know God, it must be without means; nothing foreign can come in between. When we do see God in his light it happens in private, safe from the least intrusion from creaturely things. Then we have immediate knowledge of eternal life.

"Seeing nothing, he saw God." The light that is God flows out and darkens every light. Concerning it Job says, "He commanded the sun not to shine and sealed up all the stars as with a seal." Enveloped in this light Paul could see nothing else; his whole soul was intent upon the light that is God to the exclusion of all else.

This is a lesson to us, for when we are busy with God, we mind little what goes on without.

Fourth, he saw nothing since the light that is God is unmingled, free from admixture. It shows it was the true light he beheld since there was nothing there. By light he simply means that he saw nothing with his open eyes. In that he saw nothing, he saw the divine nothing. According to St. Paul, "Who only sees being blind, sees God." When the soul is blind and can see nothing else, it is inevitable that she sees God.

A master says, the eye at its clearest, without any color, sees every color. In colorless things all colors are seen. Accordingly, it says, "He saw the nothing whose light all lights are, whose being all beings are."

The bride says in the Book of Love: "When I had passed by a little I found him my soul loves." The little she passed consists in all creatures. Whoever does not put these behind him shall not find God. She also implies that however subtle or pure a thing I know God by, it still must go. Even the light that is God, taken where it plays upon my soul, is not sufficient. I must go on to take it at the source. I cannot really see the light that shines upon the wall unless I turn my gaze to where it comes from. But if I take it in its cause I am robbed of its effect. So I ought to take it neither where it falls nor where it comes from, nor even as it abides in itself. These are all mere modes. We must take God in modeless mode and unconditioned essence, for he is free from mode.

St. Bernard says, "He who would know you, God, must measure you without measure." Pray God we may attain that understanding that is wholly without mode and without measure. So help us God. Amen.

On the Spirit

Behold the twofold emanation of divinity. One is the descent of the Son from the Father, which occurs like a birth. The second is the outpouring of the love of Father and Son in the Holy Spirit. In him, they love one another.

According to the scriptures, "The spirit of the Lord has filled the whole world." Why is he called Lord? Because he fills us. Why is he called spirit? Because he unites us with himself.

A lord is known by three signs. First, he is rich. Rich means possessing all things without restriction. Hence none is really rich but God, in whom all things are harbored indivisibly. Thus he can give all things, which is the second sign of riches. A philosopher says, God hawks himself to all creatures and each takes as much as it wants. I say, God offers himself to me as he does to the highest angel, and were I as apt as he is I would receive as he does. As I have often observed, God often behaves as though he were trying to please the soul. The third sign of riches is giving for love; whoever gives for other motives is not really rich. God's richness is shown by giving all his gifts gratis. He alone is the Lord as well as the spirit. I say he is spirit because our happiness lies in union with him.

The being of the soul receives the influx of God's light, not pure and limpid as God sends it forth, but in ambient undulations. We can see the sunlight where it falls upon a tree or any other object, but we fail to apprehend the sun itself. So it is with any gift of God: its measure is determined by the taker, not the giver.

Spirit is a subtle thing, bringing life to all the limbs of the body by virtue of the close accord of soul with body. This fact I make bold to state: because of the intimate union of the body and the soul, the soul is present in the smallest member as much as in the whole body. St. Augustine says, "The union of body and soul may be close, but closer still the the union that spirit has with spirit." Thus as God is Lord and spirit, may he beatify us by uniting us with him.

It is a puzzling question how the soul survives when God imprints himself in her. Consider. Were God to give her anything outside himself she would scorn it. But when he gives her himself from within himself, she can receive and suffer in him and not in herself, since his being is hers. So she suffers in union with God. This is the spirit of the Lord that has filled the whole world. Amen.

God Does Not Look Outside Himself

All creatures seek outside themselves, in one another, what they lack. God does not. God does not look outside himself. Everything that creatures have God has entire in him; he is the floor, the roof of creatures.

God is a simple presence, a stay-at-home in himself. With any creature, as regards her noble nature, the more she sits at home, the more of herself she gives out. A common stone, like limestone, for example, gives itself out a stone and nothing more. But a precious stone has great power because of something in it, some interior fortress from which it rears its head and peers out. According to the masters, no creature is so stay-at-home as body and soul, nor goes so far afield as the soul's highest part.

On Angels

What is an angel? Three masters give different definitions of an angel. Dionysius says an angel is a clear mirror without flaw containing the reflection of God's light. Augustine says an angel is near to God. John Damascene says an angel is a reflection of God and through all that is his there is shining the image of God. The soul has this image in her summit, where the light of God forever shines. Later on he calls the angel a dividing sword, aflame with divine desire, and he adds, "angels are free and inimical to matter."

According to Dionysius, an angel has three functions. First, he purifies; next, he enlightens; last, he perfects. He purifies the soul from stain, purging her from matter and gathering her together to herself, cleansing her as one angel does another. Then he enlightens her in two ways. Divine light is so overwhelming that the soul is unable to bear it unless it is tempered in the angel's light and so conveyed into the soul. He therefore enlightens her by reflection. The angel conveys his own knowledge to the soul and strengthens her in this way to bear the light of God.

Time and Eternity

It is an obvious fact that time affects neither God nor the soul. If time touched the soul she would not be the soul. If God were affected by time he would not be God. Further, if time could touch the soul, then God could not be born in her. The soul wherein God is born must have escaped from time, and time must have dropped away from her. She must be absolutely one in will and desire.

If someone had the knowledge and the power to gather up all the happenings of the past and all that is to come before the world ends, all this summed up into one present now would be the fullness of time. This is the now of eternity, when the soul knows all things in God, as new and fresh and lovely as I find them at present.

The narrowest of the powers of my soul is more than heaven wide. This is to say nothing of the intellect, wherein there is measureless space, and where I am as near a place a thousand miles away as the spot I am standing on this moment.

What is Conceived Where God Conceives Himself

Beatitude lies in four things. To have all that has being and is desirable and delightful; to have it all at once and whole in the undivided soul; to have it in God, revealed in its perfection and flower; to have it where it first burgeons forth in the ground of its existence, conceived where God is conceiving himself. That is happiness.

Now theologians question whether the kernel of eternal life lies more in intellect or will. Will has two operations: desire and love. Intellect, with its simple function, is therefore better; its work is understanding, and it never stops till it gets a naked hold on what it sees. Hence it runs ahead of will and tells it what to love. We desire a thing while as yet we do not possess it. When we have it we love it, and desire falls away.

Understanding is the head of the soul. The superficial notion is that love stands first. But the soundest arguments expressly state (what is the truth) that the kernel of eternal life lies in knowledge rather than love. Love turns to the loved, and finds there what is good. Intellect seizes the cause of the good. Honey is sweeter in itself than anything we make from it. Love takes God as being sweet, but intellect goes deeper and conceives God as being.

The Qualities of Intellect

Now you must realize how mightily God loves the soul. He who would rob God of loving the soul would rob him of his very life and being; he would kill God, so to speak. For the very love with which God loves the soul is the Holy Spirit. If God loves the soul so much, the soul must be a very important thing.

There is one power in the soul of prime importance in making her aware of God: intellect. It has five properties. First, it is detached from here and now. Next, it is like nothing. Third, it is pure and uncompounded. Fourth, it is self-searching, or active in itself. Fifth, it is an image.

First, being detached from here and now means from time and place. *Now* is the minimum of time. Small though it be, it must go. Everything time touches has to go. And *here* means place. The spot I am standing on is small, but it must disappear before I can see God.

Second, it has no like. A philosopher says, God is a thing that nothing is like and that nothing can become like. But according to St. John, "we shall be called God's children," and if we are God's children we must resemble God. How then can the philosopher say God is a thing that nothing is like?

The answer is that, in being like nothing, this power is like God. God is like nothing and this power is like nothing. You must understand that all creatures are by nature endeavouring to be like God. The heavens would not revolve unless they followed on the track of God or of his likeness. If God were not in all things, nature would stop dead, not working and not wanting. For whether you like it or not, and whether you know it or not, nature fundamentally is seeking God. Nature's quarry is not meat or drink or clothes or comfort or anything at all, if there is nothing of God in it. Covertly, she pursues the trail of God in things.

Third, it is pure and unmingled. By nature God can tolerate no mingling or admixture. Nor is there in this power any intermingling or admixture; it is free from impurity and nothing foreign can enter it. If someone hangs something on my cloak, and I go out wearing it, then what is attached to it goes with me, too. So, what the spirit rests on or is attached to, the spirit takes with it. The man who rests on nothing, is attached to nothing, will remain unmoved, though heaven and earth should fall.

Fourth, it is ever seeking and working within. God abides in the innermost, and intellect seeks him there. But will goes out to what it loves. So at the coming of my friend, my heart goes out to him and he is thereby glad. St. Paul declares, "we shall know God as we are known." According to St. John, "we shall see God as he is," and I can only see God in what he sees himself in. St. Paul declares that "God dwells in light inaccessible." It is not to be denied that staying in the entryway, though well and good, is yet a long way from the truth, for it is not God.

Fifth, it is an image. Take note of this, for it gives you the whole sermon in a nutshell. Object and image are bound up with one another so that we cannot part them. We can think of the sun apart from light and of light as independent of the sun. But we cannot part the object from its image. Further, even God cannot distangle them; they are born together and they die together. Cloth that is bleached is like all whiteness in its whiteness. But if you blacken it, it is dead to whiteness. And here it is the same. If an image that is God's likeness disappeared, God would vanish before us.

Now mark my words. Intellect peers in, searching every corner of the Godhead, and finding the Son in the heart of the Father, in his ground, it sets him in its own ground. Intellect presses in, not content with good or wisdom or truth or even God himself. She is no more satisfied with God than with a tree or a stone. She never rests until she gets into the ground from which wisdom and goodness come and takes them from their source, before their emergence. This ground is far higher than wisdom and goodness themselves. Her sister, will, contents herself with

God as being good. But intellect, leaving this behind, goes in and breaks through to the root from which the Son shoots forth and the Holy Spirit blossoms. May we discover this and be forever blessed.

Prepare All Creatures to Return to God

Take note: I will say something here I have never said before. When God created the heavens and the earth and all creatures, God did no work; he had no work to do; there was no activity in him. God said: "We will make a likeness." Not the Father or the Son or the Holy Spirit: we, the holy Trinity in concert, will make a likeness.

When God made man he wrought in the soul his like work, his ever-cherished, his working work. God's nature, his being and his Godhead depend upon his working in the soul. God be praised, God be praised!

God works in the soul; he is in love with his work. The work is love and the love is God. God loves himself and his nature, his essence and his Godhead. In the love wherein he loves himself God loves all creatures. With this love he loves them not as creatures; he loves creatures as God.

Again I say what I have never said before. God enjoys himself. In the joy wherein God enjoys himself he enjoys all creatures, not as creatures—creatures as God. In the joy wherein God enjoys himself, he enjoys all things. And note: all creatures tend toward their ultimate perfection.

Understand me, I beseech you, by the eternal ever-valid truth and by my soul. For yet again I say a thing I have never said before: God and Godhead are as different as earth from heaven. Moreover, I declare: the outward and the inward man are as different, too, as earth and heaven. God is higher, many thousand miles. Yet God becomes and unbecomes.

But to resume my argument: God enjoys himself in all things. The sun sheds his light upon all creatures, and anything he sheds his beams upon absorbs them, yet he loses nothing of his brightness. All creatures sacrifice their life for being. Creatures all come into my mind and are rational in me. I alone prepare all creatures to return to God. Beware, all of you, what you do.

To return to my inner and outer man. My outer man enjoys creatures as creatures, like wine and bread and meat. But my inner man enjoys things not as creatures, but as the gift of God. And my inmost man enjoys them not as God's gift, but as eternity.

I take a bowl of water and place a mirror in it and set it in the sun. The sun sends forth his light-rays both from his disc and also from the bottom of the bowl, suffering no diminution thereby. The reflection of the mirror in the sun is a sun. The sun and it are thus what the reflection is. And so with God. God is in the soul with his nature, his essence and his Godhead, but he is not the soul. The soul's reflection is in God. God and she are thus what she is. There God is all creatures. There God's utterance is God.

What is Prayer?

Stand in the gate in the house of God: stand in his unity of essence. One is best kept by itself. So the unity stands by God and keeps God together, adding nothing. There unity sits in his own presence, in his is-ness, all in himself, nowhere out of himself. But as he melts, he runs. He melts and runs in his goodness, which consists in knowledge and love. Knowledge is hotter than love, but this knowledge is laden with love. Love is fooled and caught by kindness: in love, I hang near the gate, not seeing the authentic vision. Even stones have love for the ground. If I insist on goodness, and grasp it, I shall seize only the gate, not God himself. Knowledge is better, for it is the head of love. No single thought belongs to this knowledge: wholly detached, free of self, it runs bare into the arms of God and grasps him in himself.

What is prayer? It is the practice of glorying in pure being.

But while any image exists in the soul, there is no glorying in God therein.

Things different from God do not glorify God.

Our Lord said once: "You pray, not knowing what prayer is. There will come true prayers, praying to my Father not in words, but in spirit and in truth."

But what is prayer? Dionysius said: "The mind's ascent to God—that is what prayer means." Where flesh wars with spirit, where time wars with eternity, there God is not. The soul must transcend. While there is anything above the soul, anything in front of God, the soul can never enter his ground.

When I subsisted in the ground, in the bottom, of the river and fount of Godhead, no one asked me where I was going or what I was doing; there was no one to ask me. But when I flowed forth all creatures spoke God. If I am asked, "Brother Eckhart, when did you leave your house?" then I must have been in the house. Thus do all creatures speak God.

And why do they not speak the Godhead? Everything in the Godhead is one, and of that there is nothing to be said. God works; the Godhead does no work. In the Godhead there is nothing to do; there is no activity. It never envisaged any work. God and Godhead are as different as active and inactive.

On my return to God, where I am formless, my breaking-through will be far nobler than my emanation. I alone take all creatures out of their sense into my mind and make them one in me. When I go back into the ground, into the depths, into the wellspring of the Godhead, no one will ask me from where I came or where I went. No one will miss me, for there God unbecomes.

My good wishes to anyone who has understood this sermon. Had there been no one here I would have had to preach it to the collection box. Some poor souls will go back home and say, "I shall settle down and eat my bread and serve God." Truly, I say that they persist in error, and will never have the power to strive for or to win what those others do who follow Christ in poverty and exile.

The Soul Gives Birth to Itself

Today we read in the gospel about the widow with an only son who had died. And our Lord came to him and said, "Young man, arise!" And he sat up.

By the widow we understand the soul. Her son we take to mean her intellectual nature. She was a widow in this sense: intellect was dead in her, and with it perished also the fruit of it, the Son.

Widow, in another sense, suggests abandonment. Even so must we abandon creatures. The prophet says, "The woman who is barren, more in number are her children than hers who is fruitful." So with the soul who labors spiritually: manifold are her offspring, instantly does she bear fruit. The soul that has gotten God is bringing forth fruit all the time. God is ever at work in the eternal now, and his work is the begetting of his Son.

The soul has nothing God can speak to, excepting her intelligence. Will as will is not receptive; will consists in aspiration.

Man has perennial youth in his intellectual nature; the more he acts in his intellect, the nearer he is to his birth, and a thing near its birth is young. The first issue of the soul is her intellectual nature, next follow will and then all the rest of her powers. Now he says, "Young man, arise!" The soul herself is one indivisible work; what is wrought by God in the light of the soul is more lovely than all of his work in creatures.

Above this light comes grace. Grace enters neither into intellect nor will. For grace to enter into intellect and will, they must transcend themselves. A master says, "There is I know not what, wholly mysterious, above them"—meaning the spark of the soul, the only part of her which is God-receptive. Here in this minute spark, called the spirit of the soul, there occurs true union between the soul and God. Grace never did any virtuous work; it has never done any work at all, though good works are the outcome of it. Grace does not unify by works. Grace is the inhabiting and co-habiting of the soul in God.

According to philosophers, the soul can give birth to herself in herself and bear herself out of herself back into herself. In her natural light she works wonders. She is able to separate what is one. For instance, fire and heat are one; in her intellect she divides them. Wisdom and goodness are one in God; in her intellect wisdom is never envisaged as goodness. This is because wisdom enters more into God. The soul brings forth in her God out of God into God; she is with young in her very self, by virtue of her nearness to God, of her being the image of God.

As I have often said, image as image—that is, as a reflection—is an inseparable thing. Soul as living in the reflection of God has real union no creature can sever. That is true union, and therein lies true happiness. Happiness lies neither in intellect or will; happiness lies above them both, and it is there as happiness and not as intellect, and God is there as God, and soul as the image of God. May he unite us to him in this sense, so help us God. Amen.

The Seat of Happiness

Beatitude opened its mouth of wisdom and said, "Blessed are the poor in spirit for theirs is the kingdom of heaven."

There are two kinds of poverty. One is outward poverty, and this is good and much to be commended in one who practices it for the sake of our Lord Jesus Christ, who adopted it on earth. About this poverty I will say no more. But there is another poverty, an interior poverty, and this is what our Lord referred to when he said "Blessed are the poor in spirit."

Bishop Albertus says, "By a poor man is meant one who is not satisfied with anything God ever made," and this is valid. But, taking poverty in a higher sense, we say that a poor man is one who wills nothing, knows nothing, has nothing. It is on these three heads that I propose to speak.

What then is a poor man who wills nothing? As long as it can be said of a man that it is in his will, that it is his will, to do the will of God, that man has not the poverty I speak of, because he has a will—to satisfy the will of God—which is not as it should be. If he is genuinely poor a man is as free from his created will as he was when he was not. I tell you by the eternal truth, as long as you possess the will to do the will of

God and have the least desire for eternity and God, you are not really poor.

While I yet stood in my first cause I had no God and I was my own; I willed nothing and wanted nothing, for I was conditionless being, the knower of myself in divine truth. Then I wanted myself and nothing else. What I willed I was and what I was I willed. I was free from God and all things. But when I escaped from my free will to take on my created nature, then I acquired a God, for before creatures came into existence, God was not God. He was what he was. When creatures came into existence, God was not God in himself, but he was God in creatures.

Now God as God is not the final goal of creatures. If a flea had intellect and could plumb the eternal abysm of God's being out of which it came, then not God and all God is could fulfill that flea. Therefore we pray we may be quit of God and get the truth and enjoy eternity, for the highest angel and the soul are all the same yonder where I was and willed that I was and was that I willed. Thus shall a man be poor of will, as little willing and desiring as he willed and wanted when he was not.

Secondly, a poor man is one who knows nothing. A person in this poverty is so free of any kind of knowledge that no idea of God is alive in him. For while man stood in the eternal species God, there lived none other in him; what lived there was himself. And so we say this man is as free from his own knowledge as he was when he was not; he lets God work as he will, while he himself stands as idle as when he came from God.

Now the question is: in what does happiness lie most of all? Some masters say it lies in love. Others, that it lies in knowledge and love, and this comes nearer the mark. However, we contend that it lies neither in knowledge or love, but in the one thing from which both knowledge and love flow and which itself neither knows or loves. Whoever knows this knows the seat of happiness. This has no before or after, and it expects nothing to come, for it can neither gain nor lose. It knows nothing of God's work within itself; it just is itself, enjoying itself in God-fashion. And in this sense I way man ought to be idle and free, unaware of what God is doing in him. That is the way to be poor.

Thirdly, the poor man has nothing. It has often been said that perfection means not having the mortal things of earth. This is true where poverty is voluntary. But this is not the sense I mean it in. The poverty of having nothing is the strictest poverty I will speak of.

Here I would remind you how I have often said, and eminent authorities have said as well, that one must be devoid of things and of activities, both inwardly and outwardly, if one would be a fitting place for God to work in. Now we say something else. Even if a man is bare of everything—of creatures, himself,

God—yet if it is still in him to provide God with the room to work in, then he is not poor with the strictest poverty. It is not God's purpose that man should possess in himself a place for God to work in. Poverty of spirit mean freedom from God and all his works, so that if God chooses to work in the soul he must be his own workshop, as he likes to be. Finding so poor a man, then God is his own patient and he is his own operating room, since God is in himself the operation. Here in this indigence man is obeying his eternal nature, that he has been and that he is now and that he shall be forever.

In the words of St. Paul, "All that I am I am by the grace of God." Yet here the argument soars above grace, above understanding and above desire. Nonetheless, St. Paul's statement is true. It is not that grace was in him; the grace of God worked in him, perfecting him to unity, and then the work of grace was done. Grace having done its work there remained Paul as he was. As we should say, he was a man too poor to have or be a place for God to work in. To preserve place is to preserve distinction.

Why I pray God to rid me of God is because conditionless being is above God and above distinction. It was there I was myself, there I willed myself and knew myself to make this man. In this sense I am my own cause, both of my eternal nature and my temporal nature. In my birth all things were born, and I was the cause of my own self and all things; and had I willed it I would never have been, nor any thing; and if I had not been then God would not have been either. It is not necessary that you understand this.

One learned doctor says, his breaking-through is nobler than his emanation. When I flowed out of God, then all things said, "There is a God." But this cannot make me blessed, for in it I acknowledge myself a creature. But in my breaking-through, standing passive and free of the will of God and all his works and even of God himself, I transcend all creatures and am neither God nor creature. Then I receive an impulse that carries me above all angels. In this impulse I conceive such riches that I am not content with God as being God, as being all his godly works, for in this breaking-through I find that God and I are both the same. Then I neither wax nor wane, for I am the motionless cause that is moving all things. Now God can find no place in man, for man has gained by his poverty what he eternally has been and shall remain. Here in the spirit God is one, and that is the strictest poverty man can know.

Leaving God for God

To love another as myself means that I would as soon wish his fate for good or ill, for life or death, happened to me as him, which would amount to perfect understanding.

Bearing on this subject St. Paul says, "I would that I were divorced from God forever, for God and for my friend's sake." As you know, to leave God for an instant is to leave God eternally, and to leave God at all is to endure hellish torment. Then what does St. Paul mean by wishing to be divorced fom God? Doctors debate whether St. Paul was on the way to perfection or whether he was perfect. I say he was perfect; otherwise, he could not have said this.

I will put into plain words what St. Paul means by wishing to depart from God. Man's last and highest leave-taking is leaving God for God. St. Paul left God for God: he left everything he could give or take of God, every concept of God. In leaving these, he left God for God since God remained to him in his essential self, not as a concept of himself, or as an acquired thing, but God in his essential actuality. This is no case of give and take between himself and God; it is the one and perfect union. Here man is the true man whom suffering can no more befall than it can befall the divine essence.

If everything temporal were comprehended in this one, it would be nothing else than the unity itself. Were I to find myself but for a single instant in this case, I would hold myself no more important than a worm.

God gives to everything alike. As they flow forth from God all things are equal; angels, men and creatures all proceed from God alike in their first emanation. To take things in their primal emanation is to take them all alike. If here in time they are alike, in God in eternity they are much more so. Any flea as it is in God is nobler than the highest of the angels in himself. Things are all the same in God; they are God himself.

God delights so in this likeness that he pours out his whole nature, his whole substance into it, in his own self. The joy and satisfaction of it are ineffable. It is like a horse turned loose in a lush meadow giving vent to his horse-nature by galloping full-tilt about the field: he enjoys it, and it is his nature. In just the same way God's joy and satisfaction in his likes finds vent in his pouring out his entire nature and his being into this likeness, for he is this likeness himself.

It is a question whether those angels who are dwelling here with us to serve and guard us have less likeness in their joys than the ones abiding in eternity. Is it in any sense a drawback to them to be serving and protecting us? No, not at all. Their joy and their likeness are undiminished, for the work of the angels is the will of God and the will of God is the work of the angels. If God should bid an angel go pick the caterpillars off a tree, the angel would obey him readily; since it is God's will it would be his happiness.

Being established in God's will, a man will want what is God and what is God's will and nothing else. If he is sick, he will not have a desire to be well. To him all pain is pleasure, multitude is pure and single, provided he is really in the will of God. Even the pains of hell would be joy and happiness to him. He has left himself and he is free, passive to all impressions.

Man being thus in the love of God is dead to self and all created things, and no more mindful of himself than one a thousand miles away. This man abides in likeness, in unity, and there is no unlikeness in him. This man has left the world and himself as well.

Supposing some man owned the world and for God's sake gave it up just as he had gotten it. Then God would give him back the world and eternal life as well. If there were a second man possessing merely the good intention, who thought:'"Lord, were the whole world mine—no, two of them—I would resign it and myself as well, wholly as I received it from you," God would recompense him just as if these things had been given. Another man with nothing to resign, physical or spiritual, would be the most resigned of all. He who for one instant wholly resigns self, to him all shall be given.

But to leave himself for twenty years and then to have self back again even for an instant, is never to have left himself at all. He who both has and is resigned, and casts no glance at what he has resigned, but remains firm and motionless in himself, that man is free.

On Detachment

I have read many writings of heathen sages, and of the Old and New Testaments, earnestly seeking to identify the highest virtue by which a person may come closest to God. And having studied all these scriptures to the best of my ability, I find it is none other than absolute detachment from all creatures. As our Lord said to Martha, "one thing is necessary," which is as if to say, he who would be serene and pure needs but one thing: detachment.

Our mentors sing love's praises, as did St. Paul when he said, "Whatsoever things I do and have not love, I am nothing." But I extol detachment above any love. First, because at best love constrains me to love God. Now it is far better to constrain God to me than for me to be constrained to God. My eternal happiness depends on God and me becoming one. But God is more likely to adapt himself to me, and can more easily communicate with me than I can with God. Detachment compels God to come to me, and this is shown as follows. Everything is drawn towards its own natural state. God's natural state is unity and purity, and these come from detachment. Hence God is bound to give himself to a detached heart.

Secondly, I rank detachment above love because love constrains me to suffer all things for God's sake; detachment constrains me to admit nothing but God. Suffering puts one in relation to the creatures from which the suffering comes, but detachment has no relation to creatures. Further, detachment can admit only God for this reason: anything received must enter into some environment. The environment that detachment creates is so empty that there is nothing subtle enough to be sustained there, except God. He is so simple, so ethereal, that he can sojourn in the detached heart.

The masters laud humility beyond most other virtues. I rank detachment before any meekness for the following reasons. Humility can exist without detachment, but complete detachment is impossible without humility. Perfect humility is a matter of self-abnegation; detachment leaves no room for self because it must remain empty. Therefore, complete detachment necessitates humility. Two virtues are always better than one.

Another reason that I place detachment above humility is this: humility means abasing self before all creatures, and in that abasement one goes out of oneself to creatures. But detachment rests in itself. No matter how excellent the going out, remaining within is better. As the prophet says, *"omnis gloria filiae regis ab intus"*: the king's daughter is all glorious within. Perfect detachment is without either lowliness or loftiness in relation to creatures. It has no mind to be below or above; it is minded to be master of itself, loving none and hating none, having neither likeness or unlikeness to any creature; the only thing it would be is *same*. It does not want to be either this or that. He who is this or that is something, but detachment is altogether nothing.

Here someone might object that, surely in our Lady all the virtues flourished in perfection, and among them absolute detachment. If detachment is better than humility, then why did our Lady glory in her lowliness rather than her detachment when she said: "He regarded the lowliness of his handmaiden"?

I answer that, in God there is detachment and humility as well, so far as virtues can be attributed to God. It was loving humility that made God stoop to enter human nature, while detachment remained within itself as motionless. Just as when he made man, the same humility and detachment operated when he created the heavens and the earth, as I shall show you later. And just as when our Lord chose to be made man he remained in motionless detachment, so too did our Lady know that he expected her to do the same, even though on that occasion he noted her lowliness rather than her detachment. So remaining unmoved in her detachment, she yet gloried in her lowliness. Had she but once remembered her detachment enough to say, "He regarded my detachment," it would have been disturbed. Any going forth from out of detachment, however insignificant, will always disturb it. That is why she gloried in her lowliness rather than her detachment.

I prize detachment more than compassion too, for compassion involves going out of oneself due to a lack in some fellow-creature, by which one's heart is wrung. Detachment is exempt from this; it stays within itself, permitting nothing to disturb it. In short, when I reflect on all the virtues I find none so wholly free from fault, none that so unites us to God as detachment.

The philosopher Avicenna said, "The mind detached is of such nobility that what it sees is true, what it desires befalls and its behests must be obeyed." For when the free mind is detached, it constrains God to itself, and could it remain formless and free from non-essentials, it would take on the nature of God. But God grants this to none beside himself; so God can do no more for the solitary soul than make it a present of himself. The person who is in absolute detachment is rapt away into eternity where nothing temporal affects him, nor is he in the least aware of any mortal thing; he is dead to the world, having no taste for anything earthly. This is what St. Paul meant when he declared, "I live and yet not I; Christ lives in me."

You might ask: "What then is detachment that it should be so noble in itself?" True detachment means a mind as little moved by what befalls, by joy and sorrow, honor and disgrace, as a broad mountain by a gentle breeze. Such motionless detachment makes a man superlatively Godlike. For God is God due to his motionless detachment; it is from his detachment that he gets his purity and his simplicity and his immutability. If a person is going to be like God, so far as any creature can resemble God, it will be by detachment. This leads to purity, and from purity to simplicity, and from simplicity to immutability. It is these three that constitute the likeness between man and God, and this likeness is in grace, for it is grace which draws a man away from mortal things and purges him from things corruptible. To be empty of creatures is to be full of God, and to be full of creatures is to be empty of God.

God has been standing in this immutable detachment for all eternity. And when God created the heavens and earth, it affected his detachment no more than if he were making nothing at all. I say further, that prayers and good works done by man in time no more affect the divine detachment than if they never occurred. Nor is God any kindlier disposed towards someone than if he had never enacted prayers and good works. And when when the Son in the Godhead wished to become man, and became man, and was martyred, God's motionless detachment was no more disturbed than if he had never been made man.

You might reply that prayers and virtuous deeds are all in vain in that case; God takes too little interest in them to be affected by them. And yet, they say that God likes to be entreated on all occasions.

Now realize if you can, that in his first eternal glance (if a first glance may be assumed), God saw all things as they would happen, and he saw both when and how he would make creatures. He saw the humblest prayer that would be offered, the least good deed that anyone would do, and he saw which prayers and devotions he would hear. He saw that tomorrow you will urgently entreat him. And when he grants your supplication tomorrow, it will not be for the first time; he has granted it already in his eternity, before you were ever born. Suppose your prayer is foolish or lacking earnestness. God will not deny it to you at that time; he has denied it to you already in his eternity. Thus God, who has seen everything in that first eternal glance, does not act in response to causes in time, for everything is from the beginning complete.

Yet men's prayers and virtuous works are not in done in vain. Whoever does well is well rewarded, though God does stay all the while in motionless detachment. As Philippus says, "God the creator holds all things in the course and order he has given them from the beginning." With him nothing is past and nothing future, and he loved all his saints as he forsaw them even before the world was made. Yet when there comes to pass in time the things he speculated in eternity, then people think that God has changed his mind. But whether he is wrathful or beneficent, it is we who change, while he remains the same, just as the sunshine hurts weak eyes and benefits strong ones, while the light remains the same.

God does not see in time, nor is his outlook subject to renewal. Isidorus argues this in his book on the Arch-Good. He says that people are always asking what God did before he created the heavens and the earth, and how there arose in God the new will to make creatures. His reply is that no new will arose in God, for even if creatures might not have existed before as they do now, yet they have existed from eternity in God and in the mind of God. God did not create the heavens and earth as we imagine when we say in our words, "Let them be!"; rather, creatures are all spoken in his eternal Word. Moses said to God, "Lord, if Pharaoh asks me who you are, what am I to say?" And God replied, "Say, He-who-is has sent me." In other words, He who is unchanging in himself has sent me.

Here someone may object: But was Christ in motionless detachment when he cried, "My soul is sorrowful even unto death!"? Or Mary when she stood beneath his cross? Yet much is said about her lamentations. How is all this compatible with motionless detachment?

Know that, according to philosophers there are in everyone two men. One, the outward man, is his objective nature; this man is served by the five senses, though he is energized by the power of the soul. The other one, the inner man, is man's subjective nature.

Now the Godly-minded man employs his soul-powers in his outward man no more than his five senses really need it. And his inner man only has recourse to the five senses so far as it can guide them in order to keep them from being put to bestial uses. What energy she has beyond that spent on the five senses, the soul gives to her inner man. And if he is aimed on some lofty goal, she will call in all the powers she has loaned to the five senses. Then the man is said to be senseless and rapt away, for he is carried to his object, which is either some unintelligible form or some formless intelligible.

Even as the virtuous man will now and then deprive his outward self of all the powers of the soul while he is embarking on some high adventure, so bestial man will rob his inner self of all its soul-powers to expend them on his outer man. Thus the outward man can be active while the inner man is wholly passive and unmoved.

Now there also existed an outer and an inner man in Christ and our Lady, and what each said concerning outward things was prompted by their outward man, the inner man remaining in motionless detachment. So was it when Christ said, "My soul is sorrowful unto death." And despite her lamentations, our Lady, in her inner man, stood all the while in motionless detachment. Consider the example of a door. The projecting door I liken to the outward man, and the hinge I liken to the inner man. As it shuts and opens, the door swings to and fro, while the hinge remains unmoved. It is likewise here.

What then, is the object of absolute detachment? It is neither this nor that. It is absolutely nothing, for it is the culminating point where God can do precisely as he will. God cannot have his way in every heart, for though God is almighty, yet he cannot work except where he finds readiness or makes it. I say "or makes it" because of St. Paul, in whom he found no readiness, but whom he made ready by infusion of his grace. On the basis of this, I affirm that God works according to the aptitude he finds. He works differently in man and in a stone. Here is an analogy: if you heat a baker's oven and put in some dough made of barley, some of oats, some of wheat, and some of rye, then even though the oven's heat is the same, it does not act alike on all the doughs. One will yield a fine bread, another one more coarse, and a third coarser still. The heat is not to blame; it is the material that differs.

Nor does God act alike on every heart, but according to the readiness and capacity he finds. In any heart containing this or that, there is something to hinder God's highest operation. For a heart to be perfectly ready it has to be perfectly empty, this being its condition of maximum capacity. Take another common illustration: If I want to write on a white tablet, then anything already written there, however excellent it might be, will hinder me. Before I can write, I must completely erase whatever is there. And so for God to write his very best within my heart, everything dubbed this or that must be ousted from my heart, leaving it quite without attachment. Then God is free to work his will.

Then what is the prayer of the detached heart? I answer, that detachment and emptiness cannot pray at all, for whoever prays wants something of God: either to have something given to him, or something taken from him. But the detached heart has no desire for anything, nor anything to be delivered from. So it has no prayers at all; its only prayer consists in being uniform with God.

St. Paul says, "Many run the race, but only one receives the prize." That is, all the powers of the soul compete for the crown, but it goes only to the soul's essence. St. Dionysius says of this quote from St. Paul that this race is the flight from creatures to union with the uncreated. Attaining this, the soul loses her identity. God absorbs her so that as self she becomes nothing, just as the sunlight swallows the dawn. Only absolute detachment brings the soul to this pass.

Here it is germane to quote St. Augustine: "The soul has a private door into divine nature, where all things become nothing to her." This door on earth is absolute detachment. At the height of her detachment, she is ignorant with knowing, loveless with loving, dark with enlightenment.

Again, we might cite a master's words. Blessed are the spiritual poor who have abandoned to God all things, just as he possessed them before we existed. Only a heart wholly without attachment can do this.

I will explain why God would rather be in a detached heart than any other. First, what does God seek in all things? I take the answer from the Book of Wisdom: "In all things I seek rest." Nowhere is there perfect rest but in a detached heart; therefore, God is happier there than in any other thing or virtue.

The more we are disposed to receive the inflowing God, the happier we will be; perfect receptivity gives perfect felicity. Now one can make oneself receptive to God only through uniformity with God; the degree of uniformity corresponds to the degree of receptivity. Uniformity comes of subjection to God, and the more one is subject to creatures the less one is uniform with God. But the detached heart, devoid of all creatures, utterly subject to and uniform with God, is wholly receptive to his divine inflow.

Hence St. Paul exhorts us to "Put on Christ"—that is, uniformity with Christ. For when Christ was made man, it was not a certain man that he assumed; he assumed human nature. If you abandon all things, then there only remains what Christ put on, and you have put on Christ.

Whoever has a mind to know the excellence and use of absolute detachment, let him take to heart Christ's words to his disciples regarding his manhood: "It is good for you that I go away; if I do not go away, the comforter cannot come to you." This is as though to say, you have too much love for my visible form for the perfect love of the Holy Spirit to be yours. Therefore, discard the form and unite with the formless essence, for God's spiritual comfort is intangible and is not offered but to those who despise all mortal consolations.

Listen, all good people: there is none happier than the one who exists in utmost detachment. There is no temporal, carnal pleasure that does not bring some spiritual harm in its train, for the flesh desires things that run counter to the spirit, and spirit desires things that are repugnant to the flesh. He who sows the weeds of love in the flesh reaps death, but he who sows the nourishing love-seed in the spirit reaps eternal life of the spirit.

The more man flees from creatures, the quicker their creator comes to him. Consider, all thoughtful souls! If even the love that we feel for the bodily form of Christ can keep us from receiving the Holy Spirit, then how much more must we be kept from God by inordinate love of creature comforts?

Detachment is the best of all, for it cleanses the soul, clarifies the mind, kindles the heart and wakens the spirit; it quickens desire, enhances the virtue-giving intuition of God, and separating us from creatures, unites us with God.

Take note, all of you! The swiftest steed to bear you to your goal is suffering; none shall taste eternal bliss but those who stand with Christ in the depths of bitterness. Nothing is more gall-bitter than suffering, nothing so honey-sweet as to have suffered. The most certain foundation for this perfection is humility: he whose earthly nature creeps in the lowest depths shall soar in spirit to the height of the Godhead, for joy brings sorrow and sorrow brings joy. Lord God, glory be to you eternally. Amen.

Index

Albertus Magnus, 2, 60
Angels, 42, 47
Aquinas, Thomas, 29
Augustine, 14, 17, 21, 26, 37-38, 45, 77
Bernard of Clairveaux, 44
Böhme, Jacob, 9
Buddhism, 3-4
Contemplation, 7-10
Detachment, 12, 13, 68-80
Dionysius the Areopagite, 4, 5, 23-24, 47
Gnosis, 5, 23
Grail, 37
Happiness, 60-64
Hell, 35
Images, 19-21
Inquisition, 2
Intellect, 28, 30-31, 50
Moses, 74
Mysticism, 1
Nicholas of Cusa, 3
Nothing, 23
Pordage, John, 9
Prayer, 8-9, 55-57
Rebirth, process of, 4, 24-25
St. Luke, 38
St. Paul, 21, 25, 38, 52, 63, 65, 68, 77, 78
Soul, 57-59, *passim*
Suso, Heinrich, 3
Suzuki, D. T., 3
Taulser, Johannes, 3
Time and eternity, 48
Vedanta, 4
Via negativa, 1